if
Love through me, Love of God;
    Make me like Thy clear air
Through which, unhindered, colors pass
    As though it were not there.

Powers of the love of God,
    Depths of the heart Divine,
O Love that faileth not, break forth,
    And flood this world of Thine.

A Dohnavur Book

by

Amy Carmichael

Fort Washington, PA 19034

If
Published by CLC Publications

U.S.A.
P.O. Box 1449, Fort Washington, PA 19034

UNITED KINGDOM
CLC International (UK)
Unit 5, Glendale Avenue, Sandycroft, Flintshire, CH5 2QP

ISBN (paperback): 978-0-87508-071-0
ISBN (e-book): 978-1-936143-51-1

HOW *if* CAME TO BE WRITTEN

*O*ne evening a fellow-worker brought me a problem about a younger one who was missing the way of Love. This led to a wakeful night, for the word at such times is always, "Lord, is it I? Have I failed her anywhere? What do I know of Calvary Love?" And then sentence by sentence the "Ifs" came, almost as if spoken aloud in the inward ear.

Next morning they were shared with another (for they had been written down in pencil in the night), and then a few others shared. After this some copies were printed on our little handpress for the Fellowship only; and that led to this booklet. At first when it was asked for, we felt, No, it is far too private for that. But if it can help any to understand what the life of love means and to live that life, then it is not ours to refuse.

Some of the "Ifs" appear to be related to pride, selfishness, or cowardice, but digging deeper we come upon an unsuspected lovelessness at the root of them all.

The pages in Part 2 are not meant to be read one after the other. Perhaps only one "If" here and there may have the needed word, and, leaving the others, the reader may find something in the last pages.

And in case any true follower be troubled by the "*then*

I know nothing," I would say, the thought came in this form, and I fear to weaken it. But here, as everywhere, the letter killeth. St. Paul counted the loss of all things as nothing that he might know Him whom he already knew; and the soul, suddenly illuminated by some fresh outshining of the knowledge of the love of God shown forth on Calvary, does not stop to measure how much or how little it knew of that love before. Penetrated, melted, broken before that vision of love, it feels that indeed all it ever knew was nothing, less than nothing.

It is clear, I think, that such a booklet as this is not meant for everyone, but only for those who are called to be undershepherds. And there are some of them for whom it has no word. They have already entered into that of which I have been impelled to write.

—Amy Carmichael

Part 1

ॐ

There are times when something comes into our lives which is charged with love in such a way that it seems to open the Eternal to us for a moment, or at least some of the Eternal Things, and the greatest of these is love.

It may be a small and intimate touch upon us or our affairs, light as the touch of the dawn wind on the leaves of the tree, something not to be captured and told to another in words. But we know that it is our Lord. And then perhaps the room where we are, with its furniture and books and flowers, seems less "present" than His Presence, and the heart is drawn into that sweetness of which the old hymn sings.

The love of Jesus, what it is
None but His loved ones know.

Or it is the dear human love about us that bathes us as in summer seas and rests us through and through. Can we ever cease to wonder at the love of our companions? And then suddenly we recognize our Lord in them. It is

His love that they lavish upon us. O Love of God made manifest in Thy lovers, we worship Thee.

Or (not often, perhaps, for dimness seems to be more wholesome for us here, but sometimes, because our Lord is very merciful) it is given to us to look up through the blue air and see the love of God. And yet, after all, how little we see! *"That ye may be able to comprehend what is the breadth and length and depth and height and to know the love of Christ which passeth knowledge"*—the words are too great for us. What do we comprehend, what do we know? Confounded and abased, we enter into the Rock and hide us in the dust before the glory of the Majesty of love—the love whose symbol is the cross.

And a question pierces then: What do I know of Calvary love?

Part 2

if

I have not compassion on my
    fellow-servant,
      even as my Lord had pity on me,
then I know nothing of Calvary love.

if

I belittle those whom I am called to
    serve,
    talk of their weak points
    in contrast perhaps with what I
      think of as my strong points;
if I adopt a superior attitude,
    forgetting "who made thee to
      differ? and what hast thou that
      thou hast not received?"
then I know nothing of Calvary love.

if

I can easily discuss the shortcomings
and the sins of any;
if I can speak in a casual way even
of a child's misdoings,
then I know nothing of Calvary love.

if

I find myself half-carelessly taking
lapses for granted,
"Oh, that's what they always do,"
"Oh, of course she talks like that,
he acts like that,"
then I know nothing of Calvary love.

if

I can enjoy a joke at the expense of
    another;
if I can in any way slight another in
    conversation,
      or even in thought,
then I know nothing of Calvary love.

if

I can write an unkind letter,
    speak an unkind word,
      think an unkind thought without
        grief and shame,
then I know nothing of Calvary love.

if

I do not feel far more for the grieved
    Saviour than for my worried self
    when troublesome things occur,
then I know nothing of Calvary love.

if

I know little of His pitifulness
   (the Lord turned and looked upon
     Peter),
if I know little of His courage of
    hopefulness for the truly humble
    and penitent
   (He saith unto him, "Feed My
     lambs"),
then I know nothing of Calvary love.

if

I deal with wrong for any other
    reason than that implied in the
    words,
     "From His right hand went a fiery
     law for them. Yea, He loved
     the people";
if I can rebuke without a pang,
then I know nothing of Calvary love.

if

in dealing with one who does not
    respond,
    I weary of the strain, and slip
    from under the burden
then I know nothing of Calvary love.

if

I cannot bear to be like the father
  who did not soften the rigors of
  the far country;
if, in this sense, I refuse to allow the
  law of God (the way of trans-
  gressors is hard) to take effect,
    because of the distress it causes me
    to see that law in operation,
then I know nothing of Calvary love.

if

I am perturbed by the reproach and
    misunderstanding that may
    follow action taken for the good
    of souls for whom I must give
    account;
if I cannot commit the matter and go
    on in peace and in silence,
    remembering Gethsemane and the
    cross,
then I know nothing of Calvary love.

if

I cannot catch "the sound of noise
    of rain"* long before the rain falls,
and, going to some hilltop of the spirit,
    as near to my God as I can,
    have not faith to wait there with
      my face between my knees,
    though six times or sixty times I
      am told "there is nothing,"
        till at last "there arises a little
        cloud out of the sea,"
then I know nothing of Calvary love.

* 1 Kings 18:41, margin.

if

my attitude be one of fear, not faith,
    about one who has disappointed
    me;
if I say, "Just what I expected," if a
    fall occurs,
then I know nothing of Calvary love.

if

I do not look with eyes of hope on
        all in whom there is even a faint
        beginning,
    as our Lord did, when,
        just after His disciples had
        wrangled about which of them
        should be accounted the greatest,
    He softened His rebuke with those
        heart-melting words, "Ye are
        they which have continued with
        Me in My temptations,"
then I know nothing of Calvary love.

if

I cast up a confessed, repented, and
    forsaken sin against another,
and allow my remembrance of that
    sin to color my thinking and
    feed my suspicions,
then I know nothing of Calvary love.

if

I have not the patience of my
    Saviour with souls who grow
    slowly;
if I know little of travail (a sharp
    and painful thing) till Christ be
    fully formed in them,
then I know nothing of Calvary love.

if

I sympathize weakly with weakness,
   and say to one who is turning back
      from the cross, "Pity thyself";
if I refuse such a one the sympathy
      that braces
   and the brave and heartening word
      of comradeship,
then I know nothing of Calvary love.

if

I cannot keep silence over a
    disappointing soul
    (unless for the sake of that soul's
      good or for the good of others it
      be necessary to speak),
then I know nothing of Calvary love.

if

I can hurt another by speaking
    faithfully without much
    preparation of spirit,
and without hurting myself far
    more than I hurt that other,
then I know nothing of Calvary love.

if

I am afraid to speak the truth, lest I
    lose affection,
    or lest the one concerned should
        say, "You do not understand,"
    or because I fear to lose my
        reputation for kindness;
if I put my own good name before
        the other's highest good,
then I know nothing of Calvary love.

if

I am content to heal a hurt slightly,
   saying "Peace, peace," where is
     no peace;
if I forget the poignant word "Let
    love be without dissimulation"
      and blunt the edge of truth,
   speaking not right things but
    smooth things,
then I know nothing of Calvary love.

if

I fear to hold another to the highest
    goal because it is so much easier
    to avoid doing so,
then I know nothing of Calvary love.

 if

I hold on to choices of any kind,
    just because they are my choice;
if I give any room to my private likes
    and dislikes,
then I know nothing of Calvary love.

if

I put my own happiness before the
        well-being of the work entrusted
        to me;
if, though I have this ministry and
        have received much mercy, I
        faint,
then I know nothing of Calvary love.

if

I am soft to myself and slide
        comfortably into the vice of
        self-pity and self-sympathy;
if I do not by the grace of God
        practice fortitude,
then I know nothing of Calvary love.

if

I myself dominate myself,
   if my thoughts revolve around
      myself,
   if I am so occupied with myself I
      rarely have "a heart at leisure
      from itself,"
then I know nothing of Calvary love.

if

the moment I am conscious of the
    shadow of self crossing my
    threshold,
      I do not shut the door,
and in the power of Him who
    works in us to will and to do,
      keep that door shut,
then I know nothing of Calvary love.

if

I cannot in honest happiness take the
     second place
     (or the twentieth);
if I cannot take the first without
     making a fuss about my
     unworthiness,
then I know nothing of Calvary love.

if

when I am able to discover something
which has baffled others,
I forget Him who revealeth the
deep and secret things, and
knoweth what is in the darkness
and showeth it to us;
if I forget that it was He who
granted that ray of light to His
most unworthy servant,
then I know nothing of Calvary love.

if

I cannot be at rest under the
      Unexplained,
   forgetting the word, "And blessed
      is he whosoever shall not be
      offended in Me";
or if I can allow the least shadow of
      a misunderstanding,
then I know nothing of Calvary love.

if

I do not give a friend "the benefit of
the doubt,"
but put the worst construction
instead of the best on what is
said or done,
then I know nothing of Calvary love.

if

I take offense easily;
if I am content to continue in a
cool unfriendliness, though
friendship be possible,
then I know nothing of Calvary love.

if

a sudden jar can cause me to speak
an impatient, unloving word,
then I know nothing of Calvary love.*

* For a cup brimful of sweet water cannot spill even
one drop of bitter water, however suddenly jolted.

if

I feel injured when another lays to
my charge things that I know not,
forgetting that my Sinless Saviour
trod this path to the end,
then I know nothing of Calvary love.

if

I feel bitterly towards those who
        condemn me,
    as it seems to me, unjustly,
forgetting that if they knew me
        as I know myself
    they would condemn me much more,
then I know nothing of Calvary love.

if

I say, "Yes, I forgive, but I cannot
        forget,"
as though the God,
    who twice a day washes all the
        sands on all the shores of all the
        world,
    could not wash such memories
        from my mind,
then I know nothing of Calvary love.

if

one whose help I greatly need
    appears to be as content to build
    in wood, hay, stubble, as in
    gold, silver, precious stones,
and I hesitate to obey my light and
    do without that help because so
    few will understand,
then I know nothing of Calvary love.

if

the care of a soul (or a community)
    be entrusted to me,
and I consent to subject it to
    weakening influences,
    because the voice of the world—
        my immediate Christian world—
        fills my ears,
then I know nothing of Calvary love.

if

by doing some work which the
    undiscerning consider "not
    spiritual work"
        I can best help others,
and I inwardly rebel,
    thinking it is the spiritual for
        which I crave,
    when in truth it is the interesting
        and exciting,
then I know nothing of Calvary love.

if

monotony tries me, and I cannot
    stand drudgery;
if stupid people fret me and little
    ruffles set me on edge;
if I make much of the trifles of life,
then I know nothing of Calvary love.

if

I am inconsiderate about the comfort
    of others,
    or their feelings,
    or even of their little weaknesses;
if I am careless about their little
    hurts and miss opportunities to
    smooth their way;
if I make the sweet running of
    household wheels more difficult
    to accomplish,
then I know nothing of Calvary love.

if

interruptions annoy me, and private
cares make me impatient;
if I shadow the souls about me
because I myself am shadowed,
then I know nothing of Calvary love.

if

souls can suffer alongside, and I
hardly know it,
because the spirit of discernment is
not in me,
then I know nothing of Calvary love.

if

there be any reserve in my giving to
    Him who so loved that He gave
    His Dearest for me;
if there be a secret "but" in my
    prayer,
  "Anything but *that*, Lord,"
then I know nothing of Calvary love.

if

I become entangled in any
    "inordinate affection";
if things or places or people hold me
    back from obedience to my
    Lord,
then I know nothing of Calvary love.

if

something I am asked to do for
    another feels burdensome;
if, yielding to an inward unwillingness,
    I avoid doing it,
then I know nothing of Calvary love.

if

the praise of man elates me and his
    blame depresses me;
if I cannot rest under misunderstand-
    ing without defending myself;
if I love to be loved more than to
    love,
    to be served more than to serve,
then I know nothing of Calvary love.

if

I crave hungrily to be used to show
    the way of liberty to a soul in
    bondage,
   instead of caring only that it be
    delivered;
if I nurse my disappointment when I
    fail,
   instead of asking that to another
    the word of release may be
    given,
then I know nothing of Calvary love.

if

I want to be known as the doer of
     something that has proved the
     right thing,
    or as the one who suggested that it
     should be done,
then I know nothing of Calvary love.

if

I do not forget about such a trifle as
     personal success, so that it never
     crosses my mind,
    or if it does, is never given a
     moment's room there;
if the cup of spiritual flattery tastes
     sweet to me,
then I know nothing of Calvary love.

if

it be not a simple and a natural thing
    to say,
      "Enviest thou for my sake?
      would God that all the Lord's
        people were prophets,"
then I know nothing of Calvary love.

if

in the fellowship of service I seek to
    attach a friend to myself,
      so that others are caused to feel
      unwanted;
if my friendships do not draw others
    deeper in, but are ungenerous
    (*i.e.*, to myself, for myself),
then I know nothing of Calvary love.

if

I refuse to allow one who is dear to
    me to suffer for the sake of Christ,
if I do not see such suffering as the
        greatest honor that can be
        offered to any follower of the
        Crucified,
then I know nothing of Calvary love.

I slip into the place that can be filled
        by Christ alone,
    making myself the first necessity to
    a soul instead of leading it to
    fasten upon Him,
then I know nothing of Calvary love.

if

> my interest in the work of others is
>   cool;
> if I think in terms of my own special
>   work;
> if the burdens of others are not my
>   burdens too, and their joys
>   mine,
> then I know nothing of Calvary love.

if

> when an answer I did not expect
>   comes to a prayer which I
>   believed I truly meant,
>   I shrink back from it;
> if the burden my Lord asks me to bear
>   be not the burden of my
>   heart's choice,
>   and I fret inwardly and do not
>   welcome His will,
> then I know nothing of Calvary love.

if

I avoid being "plowed under,"
   with all that such plowing entails
      of rough handling, isolation,
      uncongenial situations, strange
         tests,
then I know nothing of Calvary love.

if

I wonder why something trying is
      allowed,
   and press for prayer that it may be
      removed;
if I cannot be trusted with any
      disappointment,
   and cannot go on in peace under
      any mystery,
then I know nothing of Calvary love.

if

I make much of anything appointed,
   magnify it secretly to myself or
      insidiously to others;
if I let them think it "hard";
if I look back longingly upon what
      used to be,
   and linger among the byways of
      memory,
   so that my power to help is
      weakened,
then I know nothing of Calvary love.

if

the love that "alone maketh light of
    every heavy thing, and beareth
    evenly every uneven thing"
        is not my heart's desire,
then I know nothing of Calvary love.

if

I refuse to be a corn of wheat that
        falls into the ground and dies
    ("is separated from all in which it
        lived before"),
then I know nothing of Calvary love.

if

I ask to be delivered from trial rather
     than for deliverance out of it,
  to the praise of His glory;
if I forget that the way of the cross
     leads to the cross
  and not to a bank of flowers;
if I regulate my life on these lines,
     or even unconsciously my
       thinking,
  so that I am surprised when the
     way is rough and think it
     strange, though the word is,
     "Think it not strange,"
     "Count it all joy,"
then I know nothing of Calvary love.

if

the ultimate, the hardest, cannot be
        asked of me;
if my fellows hesitate to ask it and
        turn to someone else,
then I know nothing of Calvary love.

if

I covet any place on earth but the
dust at the foot of the cross,
        then I know nothing of Calvary love.

That which I know not, teach Thou me,
O Lord, my God.

Part 3

1

I have felt these words scorching to write, but it is borne upon me that, in spite of all our hymns and prayers (so many of them for love), it is possible to be content with the shallows of love, if indeed such shallows should be called love at all.

(Perhaps prayer often needs to be followed by a little pause, that we may have time to open our hearts to that for which we have prayed. We often rush from prayer to prayer without waiting for the word within, which says, "I have heard you, My child.")

The more we ponder our Lord's words about love, and the burning words the Spirit gave to His followers to write, the more acutely do we feel our deadly lack. The Searchlight of the Spirit exposes us to ourselves, and such a discovery leaves us appalled. How can even He who is the God of all patience have patience with us? Like Job we abhor ourselves and repent in dust and ashes.

But the light is not turned upon us to rob us of our hope. There is a lifting up. If only we desire to be purged from self with its entangling nets, its subtleties, its disguises (falsehoods truly), its facile showing of brass for gold, as the Tamil says; if, hating unlove from the ground of the heart, we cry to be delivered, then our God will be to us a God of deliverances.

2

*N*o vision of the night can show, no word declare, with what longings of love Divine Love waits till the heart, all weary and sick of itself, turns to its Lord and says, "Take full possession." There is no need to plead that the love of God shall fill our heart as though He were unwilling to fill us: He is willing as light is willing to flood a room that is opened to its brightness; willing as water is willing to flow into an emptied channel. Love is pressing around us on all sides like air. Cease to resist, and instantly love takes possession. As the 15th century poem *Quia amore langues* says,

> *Long and love thou never so high,*
> *My love is more than thine may be.*

More, far more. For as His abundance of pardon passes our power to tell it, so does His abundance of love: it is far as the east is from the west, high as the heaven is above the earth. But words fail. Love soars above them all.

To look at ourselves leads to despair. Thank God, the Blood cleanseth.

If thou be foul, I shall make thee clean,
If thou be sick, I shall thee heal.
Foundest thou ever love so leal?

Never, Lord, never.

3

Sometimes, when we are distressed by past failure and tormented by fear of failure in the future should we again set our faces toward Jerusalem, nothing helps so much as to give some familiar scripture time to enter into us and become part of our being. The words "grace for grace" have been a help to me since I read in a little old book of Bishop Moule's something that opened their meaning. (Till then I had not understood them.)

He says "for" means simply "instead": "grace instead of grace." "The image is of a perpetual succession of supply; a displacement ever going on; ceaseless changes of need and demand.

"The picture before us is as of a river. Stand on its banks, and contemplate the flow of waters. A minute passes, and another. Is it the same stream still? Yes. But is it the same water? No. The liquid mass that passed you a few seconds ago fills now another section of the channel; new water has displaced it, or if you please, replaced it; *water instead of water*. And so hour by hour, and year by year, and century by century, the process holds; one stream, other waters—living, not stagnant, because always in the great identity there is perpetual exchange. Grace takes the place of grace [and love takes the place of love]; ever new, ever old, ever the same, ever fresh and young, for hour by hour, for year by year, through Christ."

4

𝒯here is no force strong enough to hold us together as a company, and animate all our doings, but this one force of Love; and so there is a constant attack upon the love without which we are sounding brass and tinkling cymbal.

That explains why every now and then those who want to live the life of love seem to be constrained to seek the searching and the cleansing of the Spirit of God, first (it has often happened so) in the secret of our own hearts, and then together; and we know how graciously God has answered us, so that, though our word must always be "not as though I had already attained," we do, by His enabling, press onward.

There is another reason why the adversary attacks love. It is this:

Far out on our uttermost rim a thing may occur which is the reflection, so to speak, of something that was nourished in the heart of one who is in the very center. I have often known it to be so. Perhaps it was never expressed in act or word, the eye did not see it, the ear did not hear it. But spiritual influences move where sight and hearing have no place; and unlove in any one of us, or even an absence of the quality of love of which we have been thinking, is enough to cause the slow stain to spread till it reaches some soul in a moment of its weakness. And irreparable harm may result.

O Lord, forgive: Thy property is always to have mercy. Give me the comfort of Thy help again. Let it be Thy pleasure to deliver me, O Lord my God.

5

The way of love is never an easy way. If our hearts be set on walking in that way we must be prepared to suffer. "It was the way the Master went; should not the servant tread it still?" It is possible that we may be enclosed in circumstances which drain natural love, till we feel as dry as grass on an Indian hillside under a burning sun.

We have toiled for someone dear to us, but never knew it as toil. We have poured out stores of health never to be recovered, but did not know it, nor would we have cared if we had known it, so dearly did we love. And all our hope was that the one so cherished would become a minister to others. But it was not so.

And then unwillingly we became aware of a strange unresponsiveness in the one for whom nothing had seemed too much to do, of a coldness that chilled, a hardness that pushed away as with hard hands the heart that had almost broken to save that life from destruction.

Then (but only those who have gone through such a bereft hour will understand) a fear worse than any pain has us in its grip: is the love of the years slipping from us? "Father, forgive them, for they know not what they do"—is that fading from our memory? "Love never faileth"—is love failing now? Shall we find ourselves meeting loveless-ness with lovelessness?

In such an hour a poem, now many years old, that expressed a desperate prayer, burned into words:

> *Deep unto deep, O Lord,*
>   *Crieth in me,*
> *Gathering strength I come,*
>   *Lord, unto Thee.*
> *Jesus of Calvary,*
>   *Smitten for me,*
> *Ask what Thou wilt, but give*
>   *Love to me.*

Yes, ask what Thou wilt—any hopes, any joys of human affection. Any rewards of love—but let not love depart. Nothing ordinary is equal to this new call; nothing in me suffices for this. O Lord of Love and Lord of Pain, abound in me in love: love through me, Love of God.

6

$\mathcal{O}$ur dear Lord listens to the prayer that goes not out of feigned lips, and it is written for our comfort that He causes those who love Him to inherit substance, the wonderful "substance" that is "grace instead of grace," the perpetual gift of His fullness. This grace is no mere "impersonal substance," but God working in us, the Lord in action in our very springs of thought and will. God is Love; so, for us, Love is this blessed "Substance" that the children of the Father are caused to inherit.

It is the river's word again. The empty riverbed "inherits" the water that pours through it from the heights; it does not create that water, it only receives it, and its treasuries are filled, its pools overflow for the blessing and refreshment of the land. It is so with us: our treasuries of time, our years with all their months, weeks, days, hours, minutes, are filled with the flowing treasure of love that we may help others. Who could have thought of such joy for us but He whose name is Love? Now unto Him that is able to do exceedingly abundantly above all that we ask or think, according to the power that worketh in us, unto Him be glory.

7

*L*et us end on a very simple note: Let us listen to simple words; our Lord speaks simply: "Trust Me, My child," He says. "Trust Me with a humbler heart and a fuller abandon to My will than ever thou didst before. Trust Me to pour My love through thee, as minute succeeds minute. And if thou shouldst be conscious of anything hindering the flow, do not hurt My love by going away from Me in discouragement, for nothing can hurt love so much as that. Draw all the closer to Me; come, flee unto Me to hide thee, even from thyself. Tell Me about the trouble. Trust Me to turn My hand upon thee and thoroughly to remove the boulder that has choked thy riverbed, and take away all the sand that has silted up the channel. I will not leave thee until I have done that which I have spoken to thee of. I will perfect that which concerneth thee. Fear thou not, O child of My love; fear not."

And now . . .

. . . to gather all in one page:

Beloved, let us love.

Lord, what is love?

Love is that which inspired My life, and led Me to My cross, and held Me on My cross. Love is that which will make it thy joy to lay down thy life for thy brethren.

Lord, evermore give me this love.

Blessed are they which do hunger and thirst after love, for they shall be filled.

Amen, Lord Jesus.

Other books by Amy Carmichael

CLC
PUBLICATIONS
Fort Washington, PA 19034

This book is published by CLC Publications, an outreach
of CLC Ministries International. The purpose of CLC is to
make evangelical Christian literature available to all nations
so that people may come to faith and maturity in the Lord
Jesus Christ. We hope this book has been life changing and
has enriched your walk with God through the work of the
Holy Spirit. If you would like to know more about CLC,
we invite you to visit our website:

www.clcusa.org

To know more about the remarkable story of the found-
ing of CLC International we encourage you to read

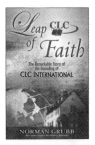

LEAP OF FAITH

Norman Grubb

Paperback
Size 5¹/₄ x 8, Pages 248
ISBN: 978-0-87508-650-7
ISBN (*e-book*): 978-1-61958-055-8

EDGES OF HIS WAYS

Amy Carmichael

Even when struggling with illness, Amy Carmichael frequently sent reflections and revelations from Scripture to missionaries and orphans within Dohnavur Fellowship to encourage them. Her collection of devotional thoughts will share with you pieces of who God is so you can better trust the completeness of His purposes for your life.

Paperback
Size 5¹/₄ x 8, Pages 234
ISBN: 978-0-87508-062-8
ISBN (*e-book*): 978-1-936143-61-0

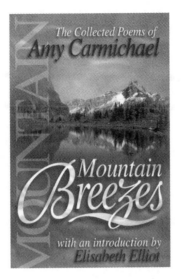

MOUNTAIN BREEZES

Amy Carmichael

Amy Carmichael was an instrument chosen by the Lord in her teenage years to minister unto the people of India. Her books have comforted and challenged many, and reveal a life and work fully dedicated to the glory of God. *Mountain Breezes* is a collection of poems that will inspire and bless readers

Paperback
Size 5¹/₄ x 8, Pages 472
ISBN: 978-0-87508-789-4
ISBN (*e-book*): 978-1-61958-098-5

PLOWED UNDER

Amy Carmichael

Amy Carmichael, admired writer and missionary, tells the story of Arulai Tara (Star of Grace), the sister of Mimosa. This book reveals the importance of preparing ourselves for obedience to God's call in our lives; the beauty in remaining faithful in preparing the ground God has given us.

Paperback
Size 5^1/$_4$ x 8, Pages 141
ISBN: 978-1-61958-082-4
ISBN (*e-book*): 978-1-61958-083-1